HANS CHRISTIAN ANDERSEN TALES

Illustrated by Gustav Hjortlund

Translated from the Danish text by R. P. Keigwin

SKANDINAVISK BOGFORLAG · FLENSTEDS FORLAG

ODENSE DENMARK

Published in co-operation with
Hans Christian Andersen Museum
Odense

Printed by Fyens Stiftsbogtrykkeri, Odense
ISBN 87-7010-091-8

Contents

Little Ida's Flowers 5

The Little Mermaid 17

The Princess and the Pea 52

The Swineherd 55

Thumbelina 65

The Emperor's New Clothes 81

Dad's always right 89

Little Ida's Flowers

My poor flowers are quite dead!" said little Ida. "Yesterday evening they were so pretty, and now their leaves are all drooping. Why is it?" she asked of the student who was sitting on the sofa. She was very fond of him, because he knew the most lovely stories and could cut out such amusing pictures—hearts with little dancing ladies inside them, flowers, and great castles with doors that opened. He was a very jolly student.

"Why do the flowers look so unwell today?" she asked once more, pointing to a whole nosegay that was quite withered.

"Ah! don't you know what's the matter with them?" said the student. "The flowers were at a dance last night, that's why they're hanging their heads."

"But flowers can't dance!" said little Ida.

"Can't they!" said the student. "When it's dark and we are all asleep, they go hopping round quite gaily; almost every night in the year they have a dance."

"Are children allowed to join in?"

"Certainly", said the student; "tiny little daisies are allowed to, and lilies-of-the-valley."

"Where do the loveliest flowers dance?" asked little Ida.

"You've often been out of town, haven't you, to look at all the beautiful flowers in the garden of the great castle where the King lives in summer? Then you must have seen the swans which swim up to you, when you offer them bread-crumbs. There are wonderful dances out there, I can tell you!"

"I was out in that garden yesterday with my mother", said Ida, "but the leaves were all off the trees, and there wasn't a single flower left. Where are they? I saw so many there last summer."

"They are inside the castle", said the student. "You see, directly the King and all his Court come back to town, the flowers at once run up from the garden into the castle and make merry. You should just see them! The two finest roses go and sit on the throne—they are King and Queen. All the red cockscombs line up on both sides and bow— they are gentlemen-in-waiting. Then come all the prettiest flowers, and there is a grand ball. The blue violets are young naval cadets, and they dance with the hyacinths and crocuses, whom they call Miss. The tulips and the large yellow lilies are old dowagers, who keep an eye on the dancing and see that everybody behaves."

"But look here", asked little Ida, "isn't there anyone to scold the flowers for dancing at the King's castle?"

"Nobody really knows what's going on", said the student. "Sometimes, it's true, the old castle-steward, who is on watch there, comes along at night with his great bunch of keys; but as soon as the flowers hear the keys rattle, they don't make a sound, but hide behind the long curtains and poke their heads out. 'I can smell flowers in here', says the old steward, but I can't see them."

"What fun!" said little Ida, clapping her hands. "But shouldn't I be able to see the flowers either?"

"Oh, yes!" said the student. "You must just remember, next time you go out there, to peep in at the windows. You'll be sure to see the flowers. I did to-day. I saw a long yellow daffodil lolling on the sofa and pretending she was a maid-of-honour."

"Can the flowers in the Botanical Garden go out there too? Can they go all that way?"

"Ra-ther!" said the student, "because they can fly, if they want to. You've seen lots of pretty butterflies, haven't you? Red ones and white ones and yellow ones—they almost look like flowers, don't they? They were flowers once, but then they jumped off their stalks high into the air and kept flapping their petals as if they were little wings, and away they flew. And as they behaved nicely, they got leave to fly about by day as well—they didn't have to go back and sit still on their stalks—and so at last their petals grew into real wings. You've seen that, of course, yourself. All the same, it's quite possible that the flowers at the Botanical Garden have never been out to the King's castle and that they have no idea of the fun that goes on there at night. Well, now I'm going to tell you something which will quite astonish the Professor of Botany who lives close by—you know him, don't you? When you go into his garden, you're to tell one of the flowers that there's a grand ball out at the castle. This flower will be sure to pass the news on to the others, and so they will all fly away. Then, if the Professor walks out into his garden, there won't be a single flower left and he won't have the slightest idea what has become of them."

"But how can the flowers tell the others about the ball? Flowers can't talk, can they?"

"No, not exactly", answered the student; "but they do it by signs. Surely you've noticed them, when it's a bit windy—how the flowers keep nodding and fluttering their green leaves; that means as much to them as if they talked."

"Does the Professor understand their signs, then?" asked Ida.

"I should just think he does! Why, one morning he went into his garden and saw a great stinging-nettle making signs with its leaves to a lovely red carnation it was saying, "You are so attractive, and I am so fond of you!" But the Professor can't bear that sort of thing, and he at once rapped the stinging-nettle over its leaves—for they are its fingers—but in doing this he stung himself and, ever since, he has always been afraid to touch a stinging-nettle."

"What fun!" said little Ida, with a laugh.

"Fancy filling a child's head with such rubbish!" said the grumpy old Councillor, who had come to pay a visit and was sitting on the sofa. He never could bear the student and always got cross when he saw him cutting out those comic figures which were so amusing—sometimes it was a man hanging from a gibbet, with a heart in his hand because he was a stealer of hearts; sometimes an old witch riding on a broomstick, with her husband perched on the bridge of her nose. The Councillor couldn't bear that sort of thing, and he always used to say just what he said now: "What rubbish to put into a child's head! All stuff and nonsense!"

But little Ida was most amused at what the student had said about her flowers, and she thought about it for a long time. The flowers drooped their heads because they were tired out from dancing all night. No mistake about it, they were ill. So she took them along to her other playthings, which stood on a nice little table where she kept all her treasures in a drawer. Her doll, Sophie, lay sleeping in her little bed, but Ida said to her: "You really must get up, Sophie, and be con-

tent with sleeping in the drawer to-night. The poor flowers are ill, and so they must sleep in your bed, then perhaps they will get well again." She picked up the doll, which looked cross and never said a word, because it was annoyed at having to give up its bed.

Ida laid the flowers in the doll's bed, tucked them well up and told them to lie quite still while she made them some tea; then they would be well enough to get up next morning. She pulled the curtains close round the little bed, so that the sun shouldn't shine into their eyes.

9

All that evening she couldn't stop thinking about what the student had told her and, now that it was time to go to bed herself, she had first to take a peep behind the curtains drawn across the window, where her mother's beautiful flowers were standing. They were hyacinths and tulips, and she whispered to them quite softly: "I know perfectly well where you're going to-night!" But the flowers pretended they didn't understand a word, and they never stirred a leaf; but little Ida knew perfectly well what they were up to.

When she had got into bed, she lay for a long time thinking how jolly it would be to see the beautiful flowers dancing out there at the King's castle. "I wonder if my flowers really went too." But then she fell asleep. In the middle of the night she woke up again; she had been dreaming about the flowers and the student whom the Councillor scolded because he filled her head with rubbish. There wasn't a sound in the bedroom where Ida lay, the night-light was quietly burning on the table, and her father and mother were asleep.

"I wonder if my flowers are still lying in Sophie's bed," she said to herself; "I should like to know!" She sat up in bed and looked over at the door, which stood ajar. In there lay the flowers and all her playthings. She listened carefully, and then it was just as though she heard a piano being played in the next room, but quite softly and more beautifully than she had ever heard before.

"That must be the flowers all dancing in there!" she said. "Oh dear, how I should like to see them!" But she didn't dare get up for fear of waking her father and mother. "If only they would come in here!" she said. But the flowers never came, and the music went on playing so beautifully that she couldn't stay where she was any longer, it was too lovely. She crept out of her little bed and went softly across to the

10

door and peeped into the next room. Oh, it was really too amusing, what she saw in there.

There was no night-light of any sort, but all the same it wasn't a bit dark, for the moon was shining through the window on to the middle of the floor—it was almost as clear as daylight. All the hyacinths and tulips were standing on the floor in two long rows; there wasn't one left in the window, where the pots stood empty. Down on the floor all the flowers were dancing round so nicely together, actually doing the Grand Chain, and holding each other by their long green leaves as they swung round. But over at the piano sat a tall yellow lily, which little Ida was sure she had seen last summer; for she remembered the student saying: "Isn't it like Miss Lena!" Everybody had laughed at him, but now Ida, too, thought that the long yellow flower really was like Miss Lena. It had just the same way of sitting at the piano, and of turning its sallow oval face first to one side and then to the other, while it nodded time to the pretty music. Nobody noticed little Ida.

Next she saw a big blue crocus jump on to the middle of the table, where her playthings were lying, and go straight up to the doll's bed and pull aside the curtains. There lay the sick flowers; but they sat up at once and nodded to the others that they would gladly come down and join in the dancing. The old smoky-top, whose lower lip had broken off, stood up and bowed to the dainty flowers, which didn't look in the least ill, but jumped down among the others and enjoyed themselves like anything.

Suddenly something seemed to fall down off the table. Ida saw that it was the teaser she had been given for the carnival; it had jumped down, because it felt it was really one of the flowers. It certainly looked fine with its paper streamers, and at the top of it was a little wax doll,

11

wearing just such a wide-awake hat as the Councillor went about in. The teaser, on its three red wooden legs, hopped right in among the flowers and stamped away like anything, for it was dancing the mazurka, and that's a dance the other flowers couldn't manage, because they were too light to stamp properly.

All at once the wax doll at the end of the teaser seemed to grow bigger and taller; it whirled round above its own paper flowers and shouted at the top of its voice: "What rubbish to put into a child's head! All stuff and nonsense!" The wax doll was the very image of the Councillor, all sallow and grumpy, in his wide-awake hat, but the teaser's paper flowers kept curling round his thin legs, and then he shrank together and became a little shrimp of a wax doll again. It was such fun to watch, and little Ida couldn't help laughing. The teaser went on dancing and the Councillor had to dance as well. It made no difference whether he grew large and lanky or remained the little yellow wax doll in the big black hat, he had to keep on dancing—till at last the other flowers, and especially those which had been lying in the doll's bed, begged him off, and the teaser stopped. At the same moment there was a loud knocking inside the drawer, where Ida's doll, Sophie, was lying among a lot of other playthings. The smoky-top ran along to the edge of the table and, lying full length on his stomach, he managed to work the drawer a little way open. Sophie sat up and looked around her in utter astonishment. "Why, there's a dance going on here!" she said. "Why didn't anyone tell me about it?"

"Will you dance with me?" said the smoky-top.

"I should think so! You're a fine one to dance with!"—and she turned her back on him. Then she sat down on the drawer, thinking that one of the flowers would be sure to come and ask her for a dance;

but nobody came. She kept coughing—ahem! ahem!—it made no difference, not a soul came up to her. So the smoky-top danced by himself, and he didn't get on at all badly either.

And now, as none of the flowers seemed to notice Sophie, she let herself fall down, plump! on to the floor. It was a terrific thud. All the flowers came running up and stood round her, asking if she had hurt herself. They all behaved so nicely to her, especially the flowers who had been lying in her bed; but she hadn't hurt herself in the slightest, and all Ida's flowers said: "Thank you for the lovely bed" and made a great fuss of her and took her along to the moonlight in the middle of the floor and danced with her, while the other flowers made a ring round them. Sophie was delighted, and told them they were quite welcome to keep her bed, as she didn't a bit mind sleeping in the drawer.

But the flowers answered: "Thank you very, very much, but we can't live very long; We've only got till to-morrow. But please tell little Ida to bury us out in the garden where the canary was buried; then we shall sprout up again next summer and be far prettier."

"Oh, no! You mustn't die", said Sophie, as she kissed the flowers. At the same moment the drawing-room door opened, and a whole throng of beautiful flowers came dancing in. Ida couldn't make out where they came from, but of course they were all the flowers which had come in from the King's castle. Two lovely roses, wearing little crowns of gold, led the way; they were the King and Queen. Next came the most charming stocks and carnations, bowing in every direction. There was a band playing, too—great poppies and peonies blowing away on pea-shells till they were purple in the face, and harebells and little white snowdrops tinkling along as if they had real bells.

14

It was such funny music. After that came a lot of other flowers, and they all danced together—the blue violets and the red daisies, the ox-eyes and the lilies-of-the-valley. And it was pretty to see how the flowers all kissed each other. At last they said good-night to one another, and little Ida also crept away to bed, where she dreamt of all she had seen.

When she got up next morning, she went straight along to the little table, to see if the flowers were still there. She drew back the curtains of the little bed—yes, there they all lay together; but they were quite withered, much more than they were yesterday. Sophie was still in the drawer where Ida had put her; she was looking very sleepy.

"Do you remember what you were to tell me?" asked little Ida; but Sophie looked very stupid and didn't say a word.

"You're very naughty", said Ida, "and yet they all danced with you." Then she took a little cardboard box, which had a pretty design of birds on it, and taking off the lid she placed the dead flowers inside it. "There's a nice coffin for you", she said, "and later on, when my Norwegian cousins arrive, they will help me to bury you out in the garden, so that you can sprout up again next summer and become still prettier."

The Norwegian cousins were two lively boys called Jonas and Adolph, whose father had just given them new bows and arrows, and they brought these with them to show to Ida. She told them all about the poor dead flowers, and they got leave to bury them. The two boys walked in front with the bows over their shoulders, and little Ida followed with the dead flowers in the pretty box. Out in the garden they dug a small grave. Ida first kissed the flowers, and then she placed them, box and all, in the earth; and, as they hadn't any guns or can-

15

nons, Adolph and Jonas fired a salute over the grave with their bows and arrows.

The Little Mermaid

Far out at sea the water's as blue as the petals of the loveliest corn-flower, and as clear as the purest glass; but it's very deep, deeper than any anchor can reach. Many church steeples would have to be piled up one above the other to reach from the bottom of the sea to the surface. Right down there live the sea people.

Now you mustn't for a moment suppose that it's a bare white sandy bottom. Oh, no. The most wonderful trees and plants are growing down there, with stalks and leaves that bend so easily that they stir at the very slightest movement of the water, just as though they were alive. All the fishes, big ones and little ones, slip in and out of the branches just like birds in the air up here. Down in the deepest part of all is the sea King's palace. Its walls are made of coral, and the long pointed windows of the clearest amber; but the roof is made of cockleshells that open and shut with the current. It's a pretty sight, for in each shell is a dazzling pearl; any single one of them would be a splendid ornament in a Queen's crown.

The sea King down there had been a widower for some years, but his old mother kept house for him. She was a clever woman, but proud of her noble birth; that's why she went about with twelve oysters on her tail, while the rest of the nobility had to put up with only six. But apart from that, she was deserving of special praise, because she was so fond of the little sea Princesses, her grandchildren. They were six pretty children, but the youngest was the loveliest of them all. Her skin was as clear and delicate as a rose-leaf, her eyes were as blue as the deepest lake, but like the others she had no feet; her body ended in a fish's tail.

All the long day they could play down there in the palace, in the great halls where living flowers grew out of the walls. The fishes would swim in to them, just as with us the swallows fly in when we open the windows; but the fishes swam right up to the little Princesses, fed out of their hands, and let themselves be patted.

Outside the palace was a large garden with trees of deep blue and fiery red; the fruit all shone like gold, and the flowers like a blazing fire with stalks and leaves that were never still. The soil itself was the finest sand, but blue like a sulphur flame. Over everything down there lay a strange blue gleam; you really might have thought you were standing high up in the air with nothing to see but sky above and below you, rather than that you were at the bottom of the sea. When there was a dead calm you caught a glimpse of the sun, which looked like a purple flower pouring out all light from its cup.

Each of the small Princesses had her own little plot in the garden, where she could dig and plant at will. One of them gave her flower-bed the shape of a whale, another thought it nicer for hers to look like a little mermaid; but the youngest made hers quite round like the sun, and would only have flowers that shone red like it. She was a curious child, silent and thoughtful; and when the other sisters decor-

18

ated their gardens with the most wonderful things they had got from sunken ships, she would have nothing but the rose-red flowers that were like the sun high above, and a beautiful marble statue. It was the statue of a handsome boy, hewn from the clear white stone and come down to the bottom of the sea from a wreck. Beside the statue she planted a rose-red weeping willow, which grew splendidly and let its fresh foliage droop over the statue right down to the blue sandy bottom. Here the shadow took on a violet tinge and, like the branches, was never still; roots and treetop looked as though they were playing at kissing each other.

Nothing pleased her more than to hear about the world of humans up above the sea. The old grandmother had to tell her all she knew about ships and towns, people and animals. One thing especially surprised her with its beauty, and this was that the flowers had a smell— at the bottom of the sea they hadn't any—and also that the woods were green and the fishes you saw in among the branches could sing as clearly and prettily as possible. It was the little birds that the grandmother called fishes; otherwise, never having seen a bird, the small sea Princesses would never have understood her.

"As soon as you are fifteen," the grandmother told them, "you shall be allowed to rise to the surface, and to sit in the moonlight on the rocks and watch the great ships sailing past; you shall see woods and towns." That coming year one of the sisters was to have her fifteenth birthday, but the rest of them—well, they were each one year younger than the other; so the youngest of them had a whole five years to wait before she could rise up from the bottom and see how things are with us. But each promised to tell the others what she had seen and found most interesting on the first day; for their grandmother didn't

20

really tell them enough—there were so many things they were longing to hear about.

None of them was so full of longing as the youngest: the very one who had most time to wait and was so silent and thoughtful. Many a night she stood at the open window and gazed up through the dark-blue water, where the fishes frisked their tails and fins. She could see the moon and the stars, though it's true their light was rather pale; and yet through the water they looked much larger than they do to us, and if ever a kind of black cloud went gliding along below them, she knew it was either a whale swimming above her or else a vessel with many passengers; these certainly never imagined that a lovely little mermaid was standing beneath and stretching up her white hands towards the keel of their ship.

By now the eldest Princess was fifteen and allowed to go up to the surface.

When she came back, she had a hundred things to tell; but the loveliest, she said, was to lie in the moonlight on a sandbank in a calm sea and there, close in to the shore, to look at the big town where the lights were twinkling like a hundred stars; to listen to the sound of music and the noise and clatter of carts and people; to see all the towers and spires on the churches and hear the bells ringing. And just because she couldn't get there, it was this above everything that she longed for.

Oh, how the youngest sister drank it all in! And, when later in the evening she stood at the open window and gazed up through the dark-blue water, she thought of the big town with all its noise and clatter, and then she seemed to catch the sound of the church-bells ringing down to her.

The following year, the second sister was allowed to go up through the water and swim wherever she liked. She came to the surface just as the sun was setting, and that was the sight she found most beautiful. The whole sky had looked like gold, she said, and the clouds—well, she just couldn't describe how beautiful they were as they sailed, all crimson and violet, over her head. And yet, much faster than they, a flock of wild swans flew like a long white veil across the water where the sun was setting. She swam off in that direction, but the sun sank, and its rosy light was swallowed up by sea and cloud.

The year after that, the third sister went up. She was the boldest of them all, and she swam up a wide river that flowed into the sea. She saw delightful green slopes with grape-vines; manors and farms peeped out among magnificent woods; she heard all the birds singing; and the sun was so hot that she often had to dive under the water to cool her burning face. In a small cove she came upon a swarm of little human children splashing about quite naked in the water. She wanted to play with them, but they ran away terrified, and a little black animal came up; it was a dog. She had never seen a dog before. It barked at her so dreadfully that she got frightened and made for the open sea. But never could she forget the magnificent woods, the green slopes and the darling children, who could swim on the water although they had no fishes' tails.

The fourth sister was not so bold. She kept far out in the wild waste of ocean, and told them that was just what was so wonderful: you could see for miles and miles around you, and the sky hung above like a big glass bell. She had seen ships, but a long way off, looking like sea-gulls. The jolly dolphins had been turning somersaults, and enormous whales had spirted up water from their nostrils, so that they seemed to be surrounded by a hundred fountains.

22

And now it was the turn of the fifth sister. Her birthday happened to come in winter, and so she saw things that the others hadn't seen the first time. The sea appeared quite green, and great icebergs were floating about; they looked like pearls, she said, and yet were much larger than the church-towers put up by human beings. They were to be seen in the most fantastic shapes, and they glittered like diamonds. She had sat down on one of the biggest, and all the ships gave it a wide berth as they sailed in terror past where she sat with her long hair streaming in the wind. But late in the evening the sky became overcast with clouds; it lightened and thundered, as the dark waves lifted the great blocks of ice right up, so that they flashed in the fierce red lightning. All the ships took in sail, and, amidst the general horror and alarm, she sat calmly on the floating iceberg and watched the blue lightning zigzag into the glittering sea.

The first time one of the sisters went up to the surface, she would always be delighted to see so much that was new and beautiful; but afterwards, when they were older and could go up as often as they liked, it no longer interested them; they longed to be back again, and when a month had passed they said that, after all, it was nicest down below—it was such a comfort to be home.

Often of an evening the five sisters used to link arms and float up together out of the water. They had lovely voices, more beautiful than any human voice; and when a gale sprang up threatening shipwreck, they would swim in front of the ships and sing tempting songs of how delightful it was at the bottom of the sea. And they told the sailors not to be afraid of coming down there, but the sailors couldn't make out the words of their song; they thought it was the noise of the gale, nor

24

did they ever see any of the delights the mermaids promised, because, when the ship sank the crew were drowned, and only as dead men did they come to the palace of the sea King.

When of an evening the sisters floated up through the sea like this, arm in arm, their little sister stayed back all alone gazing after them. She would have cried, only a mermaid hasn't any tears, and so she suffers all the more.

"Oh, if only I were fifteen!" she said. "I'm sure I shall love that world up there and the people who live in it."

And then at last she was fifteen.

"There, now you'll soon be off our hands." said her grandmother, the old Dowager Queen. "Come now, let me dress you up like your sisters"; and she put a wreath of white lilies on her hair, but every petal of the flowers was half a pearl. And the old lady made eight big oysters nip tight on to the Princess's tail to show her high rank.

"Oo! that hurts," said the little mermaid.

"Yes," said the grandmother, "one can't have beauty for nothing."

How she would have liked to shake off all this finery and put away the heavy wreath! The red flowers in her garden suited her much better, but she didn't dare make any change, "Goodbye," she said, and went up through the water as light and clear as a bubble.

The sun had just set, as she put her head up out of the sea, but the clouds had still a gleam of rose and gold; and up in the pale pink sky the evening star shone clear and beautiful. The air was soft and fresh, and the sea dead calm. A large three-masted ship was lying there, with only one sail hoisted because not a breath of wind was stirring, and sailors were lolling about in the rigging and on the yards. There was music and singing, and as it grew dark hundreds of lanterns were lit that, with their many different colours, looked as if the flags of all nations were flying in the breeze.

The little mermaid swam right up to the porthole of the cabin and, every time she rose with swell of the wave, she could see through the clear glass a crowd of splendidly dressed people; but the handsomest of them all was a young Prince with large dark eyes. He couldn't have been much more than sixteen; it was his birthday, and that's why there was all this set-out. As the young Prince came out on to the deck where sailors were dancing, over a hundred rockets swished up into the sky— and broke into a glitter like broad daylight. That frightened the little mermaid, and she dived down under the water; but she quickly popped up her head again, and look! it was just as if all the stars in heaven were falling down on her. Never had she seen such fireworks. Great suns went spinning around, gorgeous firefishes swerving into the blue air, and all this glitter was mirrored in the clear still water. On board the ship herself it was so light that you could make out every little rope, let alone the passengers. Oh, how handsome the young Prince was; he shook hands with the sailors, he laughed and smiled, while the music went floating out into the loveliness of the night.

It grew late, but the little mermaid couldn't take her eyes off the ship and the beautiful Prince. The coloured lanterns were put out, the rockets no longer climbed into the sky, and the cannon were heard no more; but deep down in the sea there was a mumbling and a rumbl-_ing. Meanwhile the mermaid stayed on the water, rocking up and down so that she could look into the cabin. But the ship now gathered speed; one after another her sails were spread. The waves increased, heavy clouds blew up, and lightning flashed in the distance. Yes, they

26

were in for a terrible storm; so the sailors took in their sails, as the great ship rocked and scudded through the raging sea. The waves rose higher and higher like huge black mountains, threatening to bring down the mast, but the ship dived like a swan into the trough of the waves and then rode up again on their towering crests. The little mermaid thought, why, it must be fun for a ship to sail like that—but the crew didn't. The vessel creaked and cracked, the stout planks crumpled up under the heavy pounding of the sea against the ship, the mast snapped in the middle like a stick, and then the ship gave a lurch to one side as the water came rushing into the hold. At last the little mermaid realised that they were in danger; she herself had to look out for the beams and bits of wreckage that were drifting on the water. One moment it was so pitch dark that she couldn't see a thing, but then when the lightning came it was so bright that she could make out everyone on board. It was now a case of each man for himself. The young Prince was the one she was looking for and, as the ship broke up, she saw him disappear into the depths of the sea. Just for one moment she felt quite pleased, for now he would come down to her; but then she remembered that humans can't live under the water and that only as a dead man could he come down to her father's palace. No, no, he mustn't die. So she swam in among the drifting beams and planks, with no thought for the danger of being crushed by them; she dived deep down and came right up again among the waves, and at last she found the young Prince. He could hardly swim any longer in the heavy sea; his arms and legs were beginning to tire, the fine eyes were closed, he would certainly have drowned if the little mermaid had not come. She held his head above water and then let the waves carry her along with him wherever they pleased.

28

By morning the gale had quite gone; not the smallest trace of the ship was to be seen. The sun rose red and glowing out of the water and seemed to bring life to the Prince's cheeks, but his eyes were still shut. The mermaid kissed his fine high forehead and smoothed back his dripping hair. He was like the marble statue down in her little garden; she kissed him again and wished that he might live.

Presently she saw the mainland in front of her, high blue mountains with the white snow glittering on their peaks like nestling swans. Down by the shore were lovely green woods and, in front of them, a church or a convent—she wasn't sure which, but anyhow a building. Lemon and orange trees were growing in the garden, and tall palm trees in front of the gate. At this point the sea formed a little inlet, where the water was quite smooth but very deep close in to the rock where the fine white sand had silted up. She swam here with the handsome Prince and laid him on the sand with his head carefully pillowed in the warm sunshine.

Now there was a sound of bells from the large white building, and a number of young girls came through the garden. So the little mermaid swam further out behind some large boulders that were sticking out of the water and covered her hair and breast with seafoam, so that her face wouldn't show; and then she watched to see who would come to the help of the unfortunate Prince.

It wasn't long before a young girl came along. She seemed quite frightened, but only for a moment; then she fetched several others, and the mermaid saw the Prince come round and smile at those about him; but no smile came out to her, for of course he didn't know she had rescued him. She felt so sad that, when he was taken away into the large building, she dived down sorrowfully into the sea and went back to her father's palace.

Silent and thoughtful as she had always been, she now became much more so. Her sisters asked her what she had seen on her first visit to the surface, but she wouldn't say.

Many a morning and many an evening she rose up to where she had left the Prince. She saw the fruit in the garden ripen and be gathered, she saw the snow melt on the peaks, but she never saw the Prince, and so she always turned back more despondent than ever. Her one comfort was to sit in the little garden with her arms round the beautiful marble statue which was so like the Prince. She never looked after her flowers, and they grew into a sort of wilderness, out over the paths, and braided their long stalks and leaves on to the branches of the trees, until the light was quite shut out.

At last she could keep it to herself no longer, but told one of her sisters; and immediately all the rest got to know, but nobody else—except a few other mermaids who didn't breathe a word to any but their nearest frinds. One of these was able to say who the Prince was; she, too, had seen the party that was held on board the ship, and knew where he came from and whereabouts his kingdom was.

"Come on, little sister!" said the other Princesses. And with arms round each other's shoulders they rose in one line out of the sea, just in front of where the Prince's castle stood. It was built in a glistening stone of pale yellow with great flights of marble steps; one of these led straight into the sea. Splendid gilt domes curved above the roof, and between the pillars that went right round the building were lifelike sculptures in marble. Through the clear glass in the tall windows you could see into the most magnificent rooms; these were hung with

sumptuous silk curtains and tapestries and their walls were covered with large paintings that were a delight to the eye. In the middle of the biggest room was a huge splashing fountain; its spray was flung high up to the glass dome in the ceiling, through which the sun shone down on to the water and the beautiful plants growing in the great pool.

Now she knew where he lived, and many an evening and many a night she would come to the surface at that spot. She swam much closer to the shore than any of the others had ever dared. She even went up the narrow creek under the fine marble balcony that threw its long shadow across the water. Here she would sit and gaze at the young Prince, who imagined he was quite alone in the clear moonlight.

Often in the evening she saw him go out to the strains of music in his splendid vessel that was dressed with flags. She peeped out from among the green rushes and, when the wind caught her long silvery veil and someone saw it, they fancied it was a swan spreading its wings.

On many nights, when the fishermen were at sea with their torches, she heard them speaking so well of the young Prince, and that made her glad she had saved his life when he drifted about half-dead on the waves; and she thought of how closely his head had rested on her bosom and how lovingly she had kissed him. But he knew nothing whatsoever about that, never even dreamed she existed.

Fonder and fonder she became of human beings, more and more she longed for their company. Their world seemed to her to be so much larger than her own. You see, they could fly across the ocean in ships, climb the tall mountains high above the clouds; and the lands they owned stretched with woods and meadows further than her eyes could see. There was so much she would have liked to know, but her sisters couldn't answer all her questions, and so she asked the old grandmother,

32

for she knew all about the upper world—as she so aptly called the countries above the sea.

"If people don't drown," asked the little mermaid, "can they go on living for ever? Don't they die, as we do down here in the sea?"

"Yes, yes," said the old lady, "they, too, have to die; their lifetime is even shorter than ours. We can live for three hundred years, but when our life here comes to an end we merely turn into foam on the water; we haven't even a grave down here among those we love. We've no immortal soul; we shall never have another life. We're like the green rush—once it's been cut it can't grow green again. But human beings have a soul which lives for ever; still lives after the body is turned to dust. The soul goes climbing up through the clear air, up till it reaches the shining stars. Just as we rise up out of the sea and look at the countries of human beings, so they rice up to beautiful unknown regions—ones we shall never see."

"Why haven't we got an immortal soul?" the little mermaid asked sadly. "I would give the whole three hundred years I have to live, to become for one day a human being and then share in that heavenly world."

"You mustn't go worrying about that," said the grandmother. "We are much happier and better off here than the people who live up there."

"So then I'm doomed to die and float like foam on the sea, never to hear the music of the waves or see the lovely flowers and the red sun. Isn't there anything at all I can do to win an immortal soul?"

"No," said the old lady. "Only if a human being loved you so much that you were more to him than father and mother—if he clung to you with all his heart and soul, and let the priest put his right hand in yours as a promise to be faithful and true here and in all eternity—

33

then his soul would flow over into your body and you, too, would get a share in human happiness. He would give you a soul and yet keep his own. But that can never happen. The very thing that's so beautiful here in the sea, your fish's tail, seems ugly to people on the earth; they know so little about it that they have to have two clumsy supports called legs, in order to look nice."

That made the little mermaid sigh and look sadly at her fish's tail.

"We must be content," said the old lady. "Let's dance and be gay for the three hundred years we have to live—that's a good time isn't it?—then one can have one's fill of sleep in the grave all the more pleasantly afterwards. To-night we're having a Court ball."

That was something more magnificent than we ever see on the earth. In the great ballroom walls and ceiling were made of thick but quite clear glass. Several hundred enormous shells, rose-red and grass-green, were ranged on either side, each with a blue-burning flame which lit up the whole room and, shining out through the walls, lit up the sea outside as well. Countless fishes, big and small, could be seen swimming towards the glass walls; the scales on some of them shone purple-red, and on others like silver and gold . . . Through the middle of the ballroom flowed a wide running stream, on which mermen and mermaids danced to their own beautiful singing. No human beings have voices so lovely. The little mermaid sang the most sweetly of them all, and they clapped their hands for her, and for a moment there was joy in her heart, for she knew that she had the most beautiful voice on earth or sea. But then her thoughts soon returned to the world above her; she couldn't forget the handsome Prince and her sorrow at not possessing, like him, an immortal soul. So she crept out of her father's palace and, while all in there was song and merriment, she sat grieving

in her little garden. Suddenly she caught the sound of a horn echoing down through the water, and she thought, "Ah, there he is, sailing up above—he whom I love more than father or mother, he who is always in my thoughts and in whose hands I would gladly place the happiness of my life. I will dare anything to win him and an immortal soul. While my sisters are dancing there in my father's palace, I will go to the sea witch; I've always been dreadfully afraid of her, but perhaps she can help me and tell me what to do."

So the little mermaid left her garden and set off for the place where the witch lived, on the far side of the roaring whirlpools. She had never been that way before. There were no flowers growing, no sea grass, nothing but the bare grey sandy bottom stretching right up to the whirl-pools, where the water went swirling round like roaring mill-wheels and pulled everything it could clutch down with it to the depths. She had to pass through the middle of these battering eddies in order to get to the sea witch's domain; and here, for a long stretch, there was no other way than over hot bubbling mud—the witch called it her swamp. Her house lay behind it in the middle of an extraordinary wood. All the trees and bushes were polyps, half animals and half plants. They looked like hundred-headed snakes growing out of the earth; all the branches were long slimy arms with supple worm-like fingers, and joint by joint from the root up to the very tip they were con-tinuously on the move. They wound themselves tight round everything they could clutch hold of in the sea, and they never let go. The little mermaid was terribly scared as she paused at the edge of the wood. Her heart was throbbing with fear; she nearly turned back. But then she remembered the Prince and the human soul, and that gave her courage. She wound her long flowing hair tightly round her head, so that the polyps shouldn't have that to clutch her by, she folded both her hands across her breast and darted off just as a fish darts through the water, in among the hideous polyps which reached out for her with their supple arms and fingers. She noticed how each of them had something they had caught, held fast by a hundred little arms like hoops of iron. White skeletons of folk who had been lost at sea and had sunk to the bottom looked out from the arms of the polyps. Ship's rudders and chests were gripped tight, skeletons of land animals, and—most horrible of all—a small mermaid whom they had caught and throttled.

Now she came to a large slimy open space in the wood where big

36

fat water-snakes were frisking about and showing their hideous whitish-yellow bellies. In the middle was a house built of the bones of the human folk who had been wrecked. There sat the sea witch, letting a toad feed out of her mouth, just as we might let a little canary come and peck sugar. She called the horrible fat water-snakes her little chicks and allowed them to sprawl about her great spongy bosom.

"I know well enough what you're after," said the sea witch. "How stupid of you! Still, you shall have your way, and it'll bring you into misfortune, my lovely Princess. You want to get rid of your fish's tail and in its place have a couple of stumps to walk on like a human being, so that the young Prince can fall in love with you and you can win him and an immortal soul"—and with that the witch gave such a loud repulsive laugh that the toad and the snakes fell to the ground and remained there. "You've just come at the right time," said the witch. "Tomorrow, once the sun's up, I couldn't help you for another year. I shall make you a drink, and before sunrise you must swim to land, sit down on the shore and drink it up. Then your tail will divide in two and shrink into what humans call 'pretty legs'. But it'll hurt; it'll be like a sharp sword going through you. Everyone who sees you will say you are the loveliest human child they have ever seen. You will keep your graceful movements—no dancer can glide so lightly— but every step you take will feel as if you were treading on a sharp knife, enough to make your feet bleed. Are you ready to bear all that? If you are. I'll help you."

"Yes," said the little mermaid, and her voice trembled; but she thought of her Prince and the prize of an immortal soul.

"Still, don't forget this," said the witch: "once you've got human shape, you can never go down through the water to your sisters and to your father's palace; and if you don't win the Prince's love, so that he forgets father and mother for you and always has you in his thoughts and lets the priest join your hands together to be man and wife, then you won't get an immortal soul. The first morning after the Prince marries someone else, your heart must break and you become foam on the water."

"I'm ready," said the little mermaid, pale as death.

"Then there's me to be paid," said the witch, "and you're not getting my help for nothing. You have the loveliest voice of all down here at the bottom of the sea. With that voice, no doubt, you think to enchant him; but that voice you shall hand over to me. I demand the best that you have for me to make a rich drink. You se, I have to give you my own blood, in order that the drink may be as sharp as a two-edged sword."

"But if you take my voice," said the little mermaid, "what shall I have left?"

"Your lovely form," said the witch, "your graceful movements, and your speaking eyes. With those you can so easily enchant a human heart . . . Well, where's your spunk? Put out your little tongue and let me cut it off in payment; then you shall be given the potent mixture."

"Go on, then," said the little mermaid, and the witch put the kettle on for brewing the magic drink. "Cleanliness before everything," she said, as she scoured out the kettle with a bundle of snakes she had knotted together. Next, she scratched her breast and let her black blood drip down into the kettle; the steam took on the weirdest shapes, terrifying to look at. The witch kept popping fresh things into the kettle, and when it boiled up properly it sounded like a crocodile in tears. At last the brew was ready; it looked like the clearest water.

38

"There you are!" said the witch and cut off the little mermaid's tongue; she was now dumb and could neither sing nor speak.

"If the polyps should catch hold of you, as you go back through the wood," said the witch, "throw but a single drop of this drink on them, and their arms and fingers will burst into a thousand pieces." But the little mermaid had no need to do that. The polyps shrank from her in terror when they saw the dazzling drink that shone in her hand like a glittering star. So she quickly came through the wood, the swamp and the roaring whirlpools.

She could see her father's palace; the lights were out in the great ballroom. They were all certain to be asleep in there by this time; but she didn't anyhow dare to look for them, now that she was dumb and was going to leave them for ever. She felt as if her heart must break for grief. She stole into the garden, picked one flower from each of her sisters' flower-beds, blew a thousand finger kisses towards the palace, and rose then through the dark-blue sea.

The sun was not yet up, as she sighted the Prince's castle and climbed the magnificent marble steps. The moon was shining wonderfully clear. The little mermaid drank the sharp burning potion, and it was as if a two-edged sword pierced through her delicate body—she fainted and lay as though dead. Then the sun, streaming over the sea, woke her up, and she felt a sharp pain. But there in front of her stood the handsome young Prince. He stared at her with his coal-black eyes, so that she cast down her own—and saw that her fish's tail had gone and she had the sweetest little white legs that any young girl could wish for; but she was quite naked, and so she wrapped herself in her long flowing hair. The Prince asked who she was and how she had come there, and she could only look back at him so gently and yet so sadly out of her deep-blue eyes; for of course she couldn't speak. Then he took her by the hand and led her into the castle. Every step she took, as the witch had foretold, was as though she were treading on sharp knives and pricking gimlets; but she gladly put up with that. By the side of the Prince she went along as lightly as a bubble; and he and all of them marvelled at the charm of her graceful movements.

Costly dresses were given her of silk and muslin; she was the most beautiful in all the castle. But she was dumb; she could neither sing nor speak. Lovely slave-girls in gold and silk came out and danced before the Prince and his royal parents; one of them sang more beautifully than all the rest, and the Prince clapped his hands and smiled at her. This saddened the little mermaid, for she knew that she herself had sung far more beautifully. And she thought, "Oh, if only he knew that I gave my voice away for ever, in order to be with him!"

Next, the slave-girls danced a graceful gliding dance to the most delightful music; and then the little mermaid raised her pretty white

40

arms, lingered on the tips of her toes and then glided across the floor, dancing as no one had danced before. She looked more and more lovely with every movement, and her eyes spoke more deeply to the heart than the slave-girls' singing.

Everyone was enchanted, and especially the Prince, who called her his little foundling. Still she went on dancing, although every time her foot touched the ground it felt as though she was treading on sharp knives. The Prince said that she must never leave him, and she was allowed to sleep on a velvet cushion outside his door.

He had boys' clothes made for her, so that she could go riding with him on horseback. They rode through the sweet-smelling woods, where the green boughs grazed her shoulders and the little birds sang among the cool foliage. She went climbing with the Prince up high mountains and, although her delicate feet bled so that others could see it, she only laughed and went on and on with him, until they could see the clouds sailing below them like a flock of birds migrating to other lands.

Back at the Prince's castle, when at night the others were asleep, she would go out on to the broad marble steps and cool her tingling feet in the cold sea-water; and then she would think of those down there in the depths of the sea.

One night her sisters rose up arm in arm, singing so mournfully as they swam on the water. She made signs to them, and they recognised her and told her how unhappy she had made them all. After that, they used to visit her every night; and once, in the far distance, she saw her old grandmother who hadn't been above the water for many years, and also the sea King wearing his crown. They both stretched out their hands towards her, but they didn't venture in so near to the shore as the five sisters.

41

Day by day she became dearer to the Prince. He loved her as one loves a dear good child, but he didn't dream of making her his Queen; and yet she had to become his wife, or else she would never win an immortal soul, but on his wedding morning would be turned to foam on the sea.

"Do you like me best of all?" the little mermaid's eyes seemed to say, when he took her in his arms and kissed her lovely brow.

"Yes," said the Prince, "you're the dearest of all, because you have the kindest heart. You are the most devoted to me, and you remind me of a young girl I once saw but shall probably never see again. I was sailing in a ship that was wrecked; the waves drove me ashore near a sacred temple where a number of young girls were serving. The youngest, who found me on the beach and saved my life—I only saw her twice. She was the only one I could ever love in this world, but you are so like her that you almost take the place of her image in my heart. She belongs to the holy temple, so that fortune has been kind in sending you to me. We will never part."

"Ah, little does he know that it was I who saved his life," thought the mermaid; "that I carried him across the sea to the temple in the wood; that I waited in the foam and watched if anyone would come. I saw the pretty girl he loves better than me"—and the mermaid sighed deeply, for she didn't know how to cry. "The girl belongs to the sacred temple, he says; she'll never come out into the world, and they'll never meet again. I am with him, I see him every day. I will take care of him, love him, give up my life to him."

But now the Prince was getting married, they said—married to the pretty daughter of the neighbouring King, and that was why he was fitting out such a splendid ship. The Prince was going off to take a look

42

at his neighbour's kingdom—that was how they put it, meaning that it was really to take a look at his neighbour's daughter. A large suite was to go with him, but the little mermaid shook her head and laughed. She knew the Prince's thoughts far better than all the others. "I shall have to go," he had said to her. "I shall have to visit the pretty Princess, as my parents are so insistent. But force me to bring her back here as my wife, that they will never do. I can't love her. She's not like the beautiful girl in the temple, as you are. If I ever had to find a bride, I would rather have you, my dear mute foundling with the speaking eyes," and he kissed her red mouth, played with her long hair and laid his head against her heart, so that it dreamed of human happiness and an immortal soul.

"You've no fear of the sea, have you, my dumb child?" he asked, as they stood on board the splendid ship that was to take him to the neighbouring kingdom. And he told her of stormy gales and dead calms, of strange fishes at the bottom of the ocean, and all that the diver had seen there; and she smiled at his tales, for she knew better than anyone else about the bottom of the sea.

At night, when there was an unclouded moon and all were asleep but the helmsman at his wheel, she sat by the ship's rail and stared down through the clear water; and she seemed to see her father's palace, with her old grandmother standing on the top of it in her silver crown and gazing up through the swift current at the keel of the vessel. Then her sisters came up on to the water and looked at her with eyes full of sorrow, wringing their white hands. She beckoned to them and smiled and would have liked to tell them that all was going well and happily with her; but the cabin-boy came up at that moment, and the

sisters dived down, so that the boy felt satisfied that the white something he had seen was foam on the water.

Next morning the ship sailed into the harbour of the neighbouring King's magnificent capital. The church-bells all rang out; and trumpets were blown from the tall battlements, while the soldiers saluted with gleaming bayonets and flying colours. Every day there was a fête. Balls and parties were given one after another, but nothing had yet been seen of the Princess; it was said that she was being educated abroad in a sacred temple, where she had lessons in all the royal virtues. At last she arrived.

The little mermaid was eager for a glimpse of her beauty, and she had to admit that she had never seen anyone more charming to look at. Her complexion was so clear and delicate, and behind the long dark lashes smiled a pair of trusting deep-blue eyes.

"It's you!" cried the Prince. "You who rescued me, when I was lying half-dead on the shore." And he clasped his blushing bride in his arms. "Oh, I'm too, too happy," he said to the little mermaid. "My dearest wish—more than I ever dared to hope for—has been granted me. My happiness will give you pleasure, because you're fonder of me than any of the others." Then the little mermaid kissed his hand, and already she felt as if her heart was breaking. The morrow of his wedding would mean death to her and change her to foam on the sea.

All the church-bells were ringing, as the heralds rode round the streets to proclaim the betrothal. On every altar sweet oil was burning in rich lamps of silver. The priests swung their censers, and bride and bridegroom joined hands and received the blessing of the bishop. Dressed in silk and gold, the little mermaid stood holding the bride's train; but her ears never heard the festive music, her eyes never saw the holy rites;

46

she was thinking of her last night on earth, of all she had lost in this world.

That same evening, bride and bridegroom went on board the ship; the cannon thundered, the flags were all flying, and amidships they had put up a royal tent of gold and purple, strewn with luxurious cushions; here the wedded couple were to sleep that calm cool night.

The sails filled with the breeze and the ship glided lightly and smoothly over the clear water.

As darkness fell, coloured lanterns were lit, and the crew danced merrily on the deck. The little mermaid could not help thinking of the first time she came up out of the sea and gazed on just such a scene of joy and splendour. And now she joined in the dance, swerving and swooping as lightly as a swallow that avoids pursuit; and shouts of admiration greeted her on every side. Never had she danced so brilliantly. It was as if sharp knives were wounding her delicate feet, but she never felt it; more painful was the wound in her heart. She knew that this was the last evening she would see the Prince for whom she had turned her back on kindred and home, given up her beautiful voice, and every day suffered hours of agony without his suspecting a thing. This was the last night she would breathe the same air as he, gaze on the deep sea and the star-blue sky. An endless night, without thoughts, without dreams, awaited her who had no soul and could never win one . . . All was joy and merriment on board until long past midnight. She laughed and danced with the thought of death in her heart. The Prince kissed his lovely bride, and she toyed with his dark hair, and arm in arm they went to rest in the magnificent tent.

The ship was now hushed and still; only the helmsman was there at his wheel. And the little mermaid leaned with her white arms on the rail and looked eastward for a sign of the pink dawn. The first ray of the sun, she knew, would kill her. Suddenly she saw her sisters rising out of the sea. They were pale, like her; no more was their beautiful long hair fluttering in the wind—it had been cut off.

"We have given it to the witch, so that she might help us to save you from dying when to-night is over. She has given us a knife—look, here it is—do you see how sharp it is; Before sunrise you must stab it into the Prince's heart. Then, when his warm blood splashes over your feet, they will grow together into a fish's tail, and you will become a mermaid once more; you will be able to come down to us in the water and live out your three hundred years before being changed into the dead salt foam of the sea. Make haste! Either he or you must die before the sun rises. Our old grandmother has been sorrowing till her white hair has fallen away, as ours fell before the witch's scissors. Kill the Prince and come back to us! But make haste—look at that red gleam in the sky. In a few minutes the sun will rise, and then you must die." And with a strange deep sigh they sank beneath the waves.

The little mermaid drew aside the purple curtain of the tent, and she saw the lovely bride sleeping with her head on the Prince's breast. She stopped and kissed his handsome brow, looked at the sky where the pink dawn glowed brighter and brighter, looked at the sharp knife in her hand, and again fixed her eyes on the Prince, who murmured in his dreams the name of his bride—she alone was in his thoughts. The knife quivered in the mermaid's hand—but then she flung it far out into the waves; they glimmered red where it fell, and what looked like drops of blood came oozing out of the water. With a last glance at the Prince from eyes half-dimmed in death she hurled herself from the ship into the sea and felt her body dissolving into foam.

And now the sun came rising from the sea. Its rays fell gentle and warm on the death-chilled foam, and the little mermaid had no feeling of death. She saw the bright sun and, hovering above her, hundreds of lovely creatures—she could see right through them, see the white sails of the ship and the pink clouds in the sky. And their voice was the voice of melody, yet so spiritual that no human ear could hear it, just as no earthly eye could see them. They had no wings, but their own lightness bore them up as they floated through the air. The little mermaid saw that she had a body like theirs, raising itself freer and freer from the foam.

"To whom am I coming;" she asked, and her voice sounded like that of the other beings, more spiritual than any earthly music can record.

"To the daughters of the air," answered the others. "A mermaid has no immortal soul and can never have one unless she wins the love of a mortal. Eternity, for her, depends on a power outside her. Neither have the daughters of the air an everlasting soul, but by good deeds they can shape one for themselves. We shall fly to the hot countries, where the stifling air of pestilence means death to mankind; we shall bring them cool breezes. We shall scatter the fragrance of flowers through the air and send them comfort and healing. When for three hundred years we have striven to do the good we can, then we shall win an immortal soul and have a share in mankind's eternal happiness. You, poor little mermaid, have striven for that with all your heart; you have suffered and endured, and have raised yourself into the world of the spirits of the air. Now, by three hundred years of good deeds, you too can shape for yourself an immortal soul."

And the little mermaid raised her crystal arms towards God's sun, and for the first time she knew the feeling of tears.

On board the ship there was bustle and life once more. She saw the Prince with his pretty bride looking about for her; sorrowfully they stared at the heaving foam, as if they knew she had thrown herself into the waves. Unseen, she kissed the forehead of the bride, gave a smile to the Prince, and then with the other children of the air she climbed to a rose-red cloud that was sailing in the sky.

"So we shall float for three hundred years, till at last we come into the heavenly kingdom."

"And we may reach it even sooner," whispered one. "Unseen we float into human homes where there are children and, for every day we find a good child who makes father and mother happy and earns their love, God shortens our time of trial. The child never knows when we fly through the room and, if that makes us smile with joy, then a year is taken away from the three hundred. But if we see a child who is naughty or spiteful, then we have to weep tears of sorrow, and every tear adds one more day to our time of trial."

The Princess and the Pea

Once upon a time there was a Prince, who wanted to have a Princess of his own, but she must be a proper Princess. So he travelled all over the world in order to find such a one, but every time there was something wrong. There were plenty of Princesses, but he could never

52

quite make out if they were real Princesses; there was always something that wasn't quite right. So he came back home and was very much upset, because he did so long for a real Princess.

One evening a terrible storm blew up. There was lightning and thunder, the rain came pouring down—it was something dreadful! All at once there was a knock at the city gate, and the old King went out to open it.

It was a Princess standing outside. But goodness! what a sight she was with the rain and the weather! The water was running all down her hair and her clothes, and in at the tip of her shoes and out again at the heels; and yet she declared she was a real Princess.

"Well, we shall soon see about that!" thought the old Queen. She didn't say anything, but she went into the bedroom, took off all the bedclothes and placed a pea on the bottom of the bed; then she took twenty mattresses and laid them on top of the pea, and then again twenty of the softest featherbeds on top of the mattresses. That's where the Princess had to sleep for the night.

In the morning they asked her how she had slept. "Oh, dreadfully badly!" said the Princess. "I hardly had a wink of sleep all night! Goodness knows what there was in the bed! I was lying on something so hard that I'm simply black and blue all over. It's perfectly dreadful!"

So then of course they could see that she really was a Princess, because she had felt the pea right through the twenty mattresses and the twenty feather-beds. Nobody but a real Princess could have such a tender skin as that.

And so the Prince took her to wife, because now he knew that he had a proper Princess. And the pea was sent to the museum, where it is still to be seen, unless someone has taken it.

There, that's something like a story, isn't it?

The Swineherd

Once upon a time there was a prince who hadn't much money, but he had a kingdom; and though this was quite small, it was large enough to marry on, and marry he would.

Still, it was really rather bold of him to say straight out to the Emperor's daughter; "Will you have me?" But sure enough he did, for his name was famous everywhere, and there were hundreds of princesses who would only too gladly have taken him. But do you think she did? Well now just listen. Growing on the grave of the Prince's father was a rose-tree—oh, such a lovely rose-tree. It only flowered every five years, and even then had but one solitary bloom. But this rose smelt so sweet that it made you forget all your cares and troubles. And the Prince also had a nightingale that could sing just as if it had all the loveliest tunes hidden away in its little throat. The Princess should have both the rose and the nightingale, he said; and so they were placed in big silver caskets and sent to her.

The Emperor had them brought before him in the great hall, where the Princess was playing "visitors" with her maids-of-honour. They never did anything else and, when she saw the big caskets with the presents inside, she clapped her hands with glee.

"I do hope it's a pussy-cat", she said . . . But then out came the lovely
rose.

"Oh, isn't it pretty!" cried all the maids-of-honour.

"It's more than pretty," said the Emperor, "it's handsome."

But when the Princess touched it she nearly burst into tears. "Oh, Papa, what a shame!" she cried. "It's not artificial, it's real!"

"What a shame!" repeated all the court-ladies. "It's real'!"

"Come, let's first see what's in the other casket before we get

57

annoyed," suggested the Emperor. And then out came the nightingale. Its singing was so lovely that for the moment there wasn't a thing that could be said against it.

"Superbe! Charmant!" exclaimed the maids-of-honour, for they all talked French, the one worse than the other. "How the bird reminds me of Her late Majesty's musical-box!" said an old courtier. "Dear me, yes! Exactly the same tone, the same expression!"

"So it is," said the Emperor; and he cried like a child.

"All the same, I can't believe that it's real," said the Princess.

"Yes, it is; it's a real live bird," said the ones who had brought it.

"All right, then let it fly away," said the Princess, and she wouldn't hear of the Prince being allowed to come.

But he wasn't going to be put off like that. He smeared his face with brown and black, pulled his cap down over his eyes and knocked at the door. "Good morning, Emperor!" he said. "I wonder if you've got a job for me here at the Castle."

"Ah, well," said the Emperor, "there are so many come and ask that. But now, let me see—yes, I want some one to mind the pigs. We've such a lot of pigs."

And so the Prince was appointed Imperial Swineherd. He was given a miserable little room down by the pig-sties, and there he had to live. But all day he sat working, and by the evening he had made a lovely little pot with bells round it and, as soon as the pot boiled, these tinkled charmingly; they played the old tune of—.

"Ah, my dear Augustine,
   our dreams are all done, done, done!"

But the cunningest arrangement of all was that, if you held your finger

58

in the steam from the pot, you could at once smell what was being cooked on every fire in the town. Well, of course, that was something quite different from a rose.

Presently the Princess came strolling along with all her court-ladies, and when she heard the music she stopped, looking so delighted; for she too, could play "Ah, my dear Augustine"—it was the only tune she knew, and she played it with one finger.

"Why, that's *my* tune!" she said. "This pigman must be a man of taste. Look here, go in and ask him how much he wants for the instrument."

So one of the court-ladies had to run in and see him; but she put on her clogs first.

"How much do you want for that pot?" she asked.

"I want ten kisses from the Princess," answered the pigman.

"Goodness gracious!" said the maid-of-honour.

"That's the price; I can't take less," said the pigman.

"Well, what does he say?" asked the Princess.

"I really can't repeat it," said the maid-of-honour. "It's too dreadful."

"Well, then, whisper it"—and the maid-of-honour whispered it.

"Oh, how rude he is!" said the Princess and walked off at once. But when she had gone a little way, the bells began to tinkle so charmingly—

"Ah, my dear Augustine,
our dreams are all done, done, done!"

"Come," said the Princess, "ask him if he will take ten kisses from my ladies-in-waiting."

"No, thank you," said the pigman. "Ten kisses from the Princess, or I stick to my pot!"

"How horribly annoying!" said the Princess. "Well, then, you ladies 'll have to stand in front of me, so that no one can see."

The court-ladies went and stood in front of her, spreading out their dresses; and then the pigman had his ten kisses and she got her pot.

Goodness! What fun they had! Day and night the pot was kept on the boil. There wasn't a kitchen in the town where they didn't know what was being cooked, whether it was the Mayor's or the shoemaker's. The maids-of-honour danced about, clapping their hands with glee.

"We know who's going to have soup and pancakes, and we know who's going to have chops and jelly. It's so interesting."

"Most interesting," observed the High Stewardess.

"Yes, but not a word to anyone, mind you; for I'm the Emperor's daughter."

"O dear, no!" they all replied. "We shouldn't dream of it."

The swineherd—that is to say, the Prince, but you see, they didn't know but what he was a regular pigman—couldn't let the day go by without making something. The next thing he made was a rattle. When you swung it round, it played all the waltzes and jigs and polkas that anybody had ever heard of.

"Now that really is *superbe*," said the Princess, as she was passing. "I've never heard anything lovelier. Look here, go in and ask him what he wants for that instrument. But, mind, no kisses!"

"He wants a hundred kisses from the Princess," said the lady-in-waiting who had been in to ask.

"The fellow must be mad," said the Princess and began to walk off. But when she had gone a little way, she stopped. "Art must be encouraged," she said; "after all, I'm the Emperor's daughter. Tell him he shall have ten kisses like yesterday, and my ladies-in-waiting will give him the rest."

62

"Oh, but we couldn't bear to do that," said the ladies.

"Nonsense!" said the Princess. "If I can kiss him, so can you. Remember, I give you wages and board"—and once more the maid-of-honour had to go in and see the pigman.

"A hundred kisses from the Princess," he said, "or we stay as we are."

"Stand in front!" she cried. And so all the court-ladies placed themselves in front, and the kissing began.

"What on earth are they all up to over there by the sties?" said the Emperor, who had just stepped out on to his balcony. He rubbed his eyes and put on his spectacles. "Why, it's the ladies-in-waiting, up to some game or other. Perhaps I'd better go and have a look"—and he gave a hitch to the back of his slippers, for he had trodden them down at the heel.

Phew! What a hurry he was in!

As soon as he came down into the courtyard, he crept along very quietly. And the maids-of-honour were so busy counting the kisses, for it had to be fair do's—he mustn't have too many kisses, nor yet too few—that they never noticed the Emperor, who now drew himself up on tiptoe.

"What's all this?" he said, when he saw them kissing; and he slogged them over the head with his slipper, just as the young pigman was having his eighty-sixth kiss. "Out you get!" said the Emperor, for he was furious, and both Princess and swineherd were turned out of his kingdom.

Look, there she sat crying, while the swineherd scolded and the rain came down in torrents.

"Poor me!" said the Princess. "If only I had accepted the handsome Prince! Oh, I am so unhappy!"

The swineherd went behind a tree, wiped off the black and brown from his face, threw away his old clothes and now stepped forward in princely robes that were so magnificent that the Princess couldn't help making a curtsey.

"My dear, I've come to despise you," he said. "An honest prince you rejected. The rose and the nightingale were not to your taste. But the swineherd—you could kiss him for the sake of a musical box. Now you can have what you asked for!"

And with that he went into his kingdom, shut the door and bolted it; but she could stand outside if she cared to and sing—

"Ah, my dear Augustine,

our dreams are all done, done, done!"

Thumbelina

There was once a woman who did so want to have a wee child of her own, but she had no idea where she was to get it from. So she went off to an old witch and said to her, "I would so dearly like to have a little child. Do please tell me where I can find one."

"Oh, that!" said the witch, "Nothing easier. Take this barleycorn—mind you, it's not the kind that grows out in the fields or that the fowls are fed with. Put in in a flower-pot, and see what happens!"

"Thank you very much", said the woman, giving the witch a shilling. She went straight home and planted the barleycorn, and in no time there came up a lovely great flower which looked just like a tulip, only the petals were shut tight as though it were still in bud.

"It *is* a pretty flower", said the woman, and she gave the lovely red and yellow petals a kiss; but directly she kissed it, the flower burst open with a pop. It was a real tulip—that was plain enough now—but, sitting on the green pistil in the middle of the flower, was a tiny little girl. She was delicately pretty and no taller than your thumb, so she was given the name of Thumbelina.

A nicely varnished walnut-shell did for her cradle, blue violet petals for her mattress, and a rose-leaf for her counterpane. That was where

65

she slept at night; but in the daytime she played about on the table, where the woman had put a plate with a wreath of flowers. These dipped their stalks down into the water, in the middle of which floated a large tulip petal where Thumbelina could sit and row herself from one side of the plate to the other, using a couple of white horsehairs as oars. It was a most charming sight. She could sing, too, in the sweetest little voice you ever heard.

One night, as she lay in her pretty bed, a hideous toad came hopping in through a broken pane in the window. It was a great ugly slimy toad, and it jumped staight down on to the table where Thumbelina was lying asleep under her red rose-leaf.

"She would make a nice wife for my son", thought the toad, and she snatched up the walnut-shell in which Thumbelina was sleeping and hopped off with her through the window into the garden.

There was a wide brook running through it, but the bank was swampy and muddy, and here the toad lived with her son. Ugh! wasn't he ugly and horrible—just like his mother! "Koax, koax, brekke-ke-kex!" was all he could say, when he saw the pretty little girl in the walnut-shell.

"Sh! Not so loud, or you'll wake her," said the old toad. "She might yet run away from us, for she's as light as swan's-down. Let's put her out in the brook on one of those broad water-lilies. She's so small and light that its leaf will be like an island for her. She can't escape from there, and in the meantime we'll get the best room ready under the mud for you two to live in."

There were quite a lot of water-lilies growing on the water with their broad green leaves which seem to be floating on the surface. The biggest of them all happened to be the furthest away, but the old toad swam

66

out and placed the walnut-shell on it with Thumbelina still sleeping inside.

Early the next morning the poor little thing woke up and, when she saw where she was, she began to cry bitterly, for the big green leaf had water all round it and she couldn't possibly reach the bank.

The old toad stayed down in the mud and decorated her room with rushes and yellow water-lilies, so as to make everything quite snug for her new daughter-in-law. Then she swam out with her son to the water-lily where Thumbelina was standing, for they wanted to fetch that fine walnut bed and put it up in the bridal·chamber before she came herself. The old toad made a low curtsey to her in the water and said, "Here's my son—he's to be your husband. You'll have a lovely home together down in the mud."

"Koax- koax, brekke-ke-kex!" was all that the son could say.

Then they took the pretty little bed and swam away with it. But Thumbelina sat all alone on the green leaf and cried, for she didn't want to live with the horrible toad or to marry her ugly son. The little fishes, swimming down there in the water, had caught sight of the toad and heard what she said. So they poked their heads out of the water; they were so anxious to have a look at the little girl. Directly they saw her, they found her charming, and they couldn't bear to think that she must go and live with the ugly toad. No, that must never happen! They all swarmed together down in the water round the green stalk that held the leaf she was standing on and gnawed it through with their teeth; whereupon the leaf floated away with Thumbelina down the brook, far away where the toad could never reach her.

Thumbelina went sailing past all sorts of places, and the little birds perched in the bushes saw her and trilled out, "What a pretty little lady!" The leaf that carried her floated further and further on; and thus it was that Thumbelina began her journey abroad.

A dainty little white butterfly kept on fluttering round and round her, till at last it settled on the leaf, for it had taken a great liking to Thumbelina; and she too was pleased, because the toad couldn't reach her now and she was sailing through such a lovely part of the brook. The sunshine gleamed on the water like the finest gold. Then she took her sash and tied one end of it round the butterfly, while the other end she made fast to the leaf; and this at once gathered speed—and so did Thumbelina because, you see, she was standing on the leaf. Just then a large cockchafer came flying up and, catching sight of her, clutched her round her slender waist and flew with her up into a tree.

But the green leaf went floating on and the butterfly with it, because it had been tied to the leaf and couldn't manage to free itself.

Gracious, what a fright it gave poor Thumbelina, when the cockchafer flew up into the tree with her! Still, what upset her even more was the thought of the pretty white butterfly that she had tied to the leaf; for, unless it could manage to free itself, it would certainly starve to death. But that didn't worry the cockchafer in the slightest. He settled beside her on the largest green leaf in the tree, gave her some nectar from the blossoms and said how pretty she was, although she wasn't a bit like a cockchafer. Later on, all the other cockchafers living in the tree came to call on her. They stared at Thumbelina, and the young lady cockchafers shrugged their feelers—"Why, she's only got two legs", they said. "What a pitiable sight!" "She hasn't any feelers", they went on. "She's so pinched in at the waist—ugh! she might almost be a human. Isn't she ugly!" exclaimed all the lady cockchafers. And yet Thumbelina was really so pretty. And that's what the cockchafer thought who had carried her off; but when all the others kept saying how ugly she was, then at length he thought so too and would have nothing to do with her; she could go where she liked. They flew with her down from the tree and sat her on a daisy. There she cried and cried, because she was so ugly that the cockchafers wouldn't have her; and all the time she was as beautiful as can be—as exquisite as the loveliest rose-petal.

Right through the summer poor Thumbelina lived quite alone in that enormous wood. She took blades of grass and plaited herself a bed, which she hung under a large dockleaf, so as to be out of the rain. She got her food from the honey in the flowers, and her drink from the morning dew on the leaves; and in this way summer and autumn went by. But now came winter—the long, cold winter. All the birds that had sung to her so beautifully now flew away; the trees and flowers withered; the great dock-leaf she had been living under furled itself into nothing but a faded yellow stalk. She felt the cold most terribly, for her clothes were by this time in tatters, and she herself was so tiny and delicate, poor Thumbelina, that she would surely be frozen to death. It began snowing, and every snowflake that fell on her was like a whole shovelful being thrown on us, for we are quite big and she was no taller than your thumb. So she wrapped herself up in a dead leaf, but there was no warmth in that, and she shivered with cold.

On the fringe of the wood where she had now come to was a large cornfield; but the corn had long been harvested, and only the bare barren stubble thrust up from the frozen earth. It was just like an entire forest for her to walk through—oh, and she was shivering with cold! At length she came to the field-mouse's door. It was a little hole down below the stubble. There the field-mouse had a fine snug place to live in, with a whole roomful of corn and a splendid kitchen and dining-room. Poor Thumbelina stood just inside the door like any other wretched beggar-girl and asked for a little bit of barley-corn, for she hadn't had a scrap to eat for two days.

"You poor mite!" said the field-mouse, for at heart she was a kind old thing. "Come you in and have a bite with me in my warm room."

As she at once took a liking to Thumbelina she made a suggestion. "You're quite welcome to stay with me for the winter," she said, "as long as you'll keep my rooms nice and tidy and also tell me stories, for I'm so fond of stories." And Thumbelina did what the kind old field-mouse asked for and was extremely comfortable there.

"I dare say we shall have a visitor before long", said the field-mouse.

70

"My neighbour generally pays me a call once a week. His house is even snugger than mine, with goodsized rooms, and he wears such a lovely black velvet coat. If only you could get him for a husband, you'd be comfortably off. But his sight's very bad. You must tell him all the nicest stories you know".

Thumbelina took no notice of all this; she had no intention of marrying the neighbour, for he was a mole. He came and called in his black velvet coat. He was so rich and clever, according to the field-mouse, and his home was twenty times the size of the field-mouse's. He was very learned, but he couldn't bear sunshine and pretty flowers; he said all sorts of nasty things about them, never having seen them. Thumbelina had to sing, and she sang both "Ladybird, ladybird, fly away home" and "Ring-a-ring-o'roses"; and the mole fell in love with her because of her pretty voice, but he didn't say anything—he was much too cautious a man for that.

He had lately dug a long passage for himself through the earth, leading from his house to theirs. Here the field-mouse and Thumbelina were invited to stroll whenever they cared to. But he told them not to be afraid of the dead bird lying in the passage; it was a whole bird with beak and feathers, that had evidently only just died as the winter began and was now buried in the very spot where he had made his underground passage.

The mole took a bit of touchwood in his mouth—for in the dark that shines just like fire— and went ahead to give them a light in the long dark passage. When they came to where the dead bird was lying, the mole tilted his broad snout up to the ceiling and thrust through the earth; making a large hole through which the light could penetrate. In the middle of the floor lay a dead swallow with its pretty wings folded close in to its sides, and head and legs tucked in beneath its feathers. The poor bird must have died of cold. Thumbelina felt so sory for it; she was very fond of all the little birds that had sung and twittered for her so sweetly right through the summer. But the mole kicked at it with his stumpy legs, saying, "That won't chirp any more! How wretched it must be to be born a little bird! Thank goodness no child of mine ever will be. A bird like that has of course nothing but its twitter and is bound to starve to death when winter comes."

"Just what I'd expect to hear from a sensible man like you", said the field-mouse. "What has a bird to show for all its twittering, when winter comes? It must starve and freeze. But I suppose that's considered a great thing."

Thumbelina didn't say a word, but when the other two turned their backs on the bird, she stooped down and, smoothing aside the feathers that lay over its head, she kissed its closed eyes. "Who knows—this may be the very one", she thought, "that used to sing so beautifully to me last summer."

The mole now filled in the hole where the daylight shone through and saw the two ladies home. But that night Thumbelina simply couldn't sleep; so she got up and plaited a fine big blanket of hay, which she carried down and spread all over the dead bird, and she took some soft cotton-wool she had found in the field-mouse's room and tucked this in at the sides, so that the bird might lie warm in the cold earth.

"Goodbye, you lovely little bird," she said. "Goodbye, and thank you for your beautiful singing last summer, when all the trees were green and the sun was so bright and warm". Then she laid her head up against the bird's breast—but at the same moment she got such a fright, for she heard a kind of thumping inside. It was the bird's heart. The bird wasn't dead; it had been lying numb and unconscious and now, as it grew warm again, it revived.

You see, in autumn the swallows all fly away to the warm countries, but if there's one that lags behind it gets so cold that it falls down dead. There it lies, where it fell, and the cold snow covers it over.

Thumbelina was all of a tremble from the fright she had, for the bird was of course an immense great creature beside her, who was no taller than your thumb. However, she took courage and tucked the cottonwool still more closely round the poor swallow and fetched a curled mint leaf that she had been using herself for a counterpane and spread this over the bird's head.

The following night she again stole down to the bird, and this time it had quite revived; but it was so feeble that it could only open its eyes for a short moment to look at Thumbelina, standing there with a bit of touchwood in her hand, for she had no other light.

"Thank you, my darling child," said the sick swallow. "I'm lovely and warm now. I shall soon get back my strength and be able to fly again, out in the warm sunshine."

"Ah, but it's so cold out of doors", she said. "It's snowing and freezing. Stay in your warm bed; I'll look after you all right."

Then she brought the swallow some water, in the petal of a flower, and the bird drank it and told her how it had torn one of its wings on a bramble and therefore couldn't fly as fast as the other swallows when they flew far, far away to the warm countries. At last it had fallen to the ground, but it couldn't remember anything after that and had no idea how it came to be where it was.

The swallow now remained here all through the winter, and Thumbelina took care of it and grew very fond of it. Neither the mole nor the field-mouse heard anything at all about this; they had no liking for the poor wretched swallow.

As soon as spring had arrived and the sun had begun to warm the earth, the swallow said goodbye to Thumbelina, who opened up the hole that the mole had made in the roof of the passage. The sun came shining in so pleasantly, and the swallow asked if she would like to come too; she could sit on its back, and they would fly far out into the green forest. But Thumbelina knew that it would grieve the old field-mouse, if she left her like that.

"No, I can't", said Thumbelina. "Goodbye, goodbye, you dear kind girl", said the swallow, as it flew into the open sunshine. Thumbelina gazed after it with tears in her eyes, for she was so fond of the poor swallow.

"Tweet-tweet!" sang the bird and flew off into the woods . . .

Thumbelina felt so sad. She was never allowed to go out into the

74

warm sunshine. The corn that had been sown in the field above the
field-mouse's home was certainly very tall; so that it was like a dense
wood for the poor little girl, who after all was only an inch high.

"You will have to start making your wedding trousseau this summer," the field-mouse told her, because by now their neighbour, the
tiresome tedious mole in the black velvet coat, had proposed to her.
"You'll need to have both woollens and linen—-something for every
occasion—when you're married to the mole."

So Thumbelina had to spin from a distaff, and the field-mouse en-
gaged four spiders to spin and weave day and night. Every evening

there was a visit from the mole, who always kept on about how, when summer was over, the sun wasn't nearly so warm, whereas now it scorched the earth till it was as hard as a stone. Yes, and when the summer had ended there was to be his wedding with Thumbelina. But she wasn't at all pleased, for she found the mole such a terrible bore. Every morning, as the sun rose, and every evening as it set, she stole out to the door, and when the wind parted the ears of corn so that she could see the blue sky, she thought how lovely and bright it was out there and did so wish she could catch sight of the dear swallow once more; but the bird never came again and had evidently flown far off into the beautiful green forest.

Now it was autumn, and Thumbelina had the whole of her trousseau ready.

"Your wedding will be in four weeks' time", the field-mouse told her. But Thumbelina wept and said she wouldn't marry the tedious mole.

"Hoity-toity!" said the field-mouse. "Don't you be so pig-headed, or I'll bite you with my white teeth. Why, he's a splendid husband for you. The Queen herself hasn't anything like his black velvet coat. His kitchen and cellar are both of the best. You ought to thank Heaven he's yours."

The wedding-day arrived. The mole was already there to fetch Thumbelina. She would have to live with him deep down under the earth and never come out into the warm sunshine, for he didn't care for that. The poor child was very sad at having to say goodbye to the beautiful sun, which she had at least been allowed to look at from the doorway when she was living with the field-mouse.

"Goodbye, bright sun!" she said and, stretching out her arms to it, she also took a few steps out from the field-mouse's dwelling; for the harvest was in, and nothing was left but the dry stubble. "Goodbye, goodbye", she said, throwing her tiny arms round a little red flower standing near. "Remenber me to the dear swallow, if you happen to see it."

"Tweet-tweet!" she heard suddenly over her head. She looked up, and there was the swallow just passing. How delighted it was to see Thumbelina! She told the bird how she disliked having to marry the ugly mole and to live deep down under the earth where the sun never shone. She couldn't help crying at the thought.

"The cold winter will soon be here", said the swallow. "I'm going far away to the warm countries. Will you come with me? You can sit on my back. Just tie yourself on with your sash, and away we'll fly from the ugly mole and his dingy house, far away across the mountains, to the warm countries, where the sun shines more brightly than it does here and there's always summer with its lovely flowers. Dear little Thumbelina, do come with me—you who saved my life when I lay frozen stiff in that dismal cellar."

"Yes, I'll come with you", said Thumbelina. She climbed on to the bird's back, setting her feet on its outstretched wings and tieing her sash to one of the strongest feathers. Then the swallow flew high up into the air, over lake and forest, high up over the great mountains of eternal snow. Thumbelina shivered in the cold air, but then she snuggled in under the bird's warm feathers, merely poking out her little head to look at all the loveliness stretched out beneath her.

And at last they reached the warm countries. The sun was shining there much more brightly than with us, and the sky looked twice as far off. On walls and slopes grew the finest black and white grapes, in the woods hung lemons and oranges; the air smelt sweetly of myrtle and curled mint, and the most delightful children darted about on the roads playing with large gay-coloured butterflies. But the swallow kept flying on and on, and the country became more and more beautiful, till at last they came upon an ancient palace of glittering white marble standing among vivid green trees beside a blue lake. Vines went curling up round the tall pillars, and right at the top were a number of swallow's nests. One of these was the home of the swallow that had brought Thumbelina on its back.

"Here's my house", cried the swallow. "But you see those beautiful flowers growing down there? You shall now choose one of them yourself, and then I'll put you on it, and you can make yourself as cosy as you like.

"That will be lovely", she said, clapping her little hands.

A large white marble column was lying there on the ground just as it had fallen and broken into three pieces, but in among these were growing the most beautiful white flowers. The swallow flew down with Thumbelina and placed her on one of the broad petals—but what a surprise she got! There in the middle of the flower sat a little man as white and transparent as if he had been made of glass. He wore the neatest little gold crown on his head and the most exquisite wings on his shoulders; he himself was no bigger than Thumbelina. He was the guardian spirit of the flower. Each flower had just such a little man or woman living in it, but this one was King of them all.

"Goodness, how handsome he is!" whispered Thumbelina to the swallow. The little monarch was very frightened of the swallow, which of course seemed a gigantic bird beside one so small and delicate as himself; but when he caught sight of Thumbelina he was enchanted, for she was much the prettiest little lady he had ever seen. So he took the

gold crown off his head and placed it on hers. At the same time he asked her what her name was and whether she would be his wife; if so, she would become Queen of all the flowers. Well, he would be a proper husband for her, quite different from the son of the old toad and from the mole with the black velvet coat. So she said yes to the handsome King, and from every flower there appeared a lady or a gentleman that was the most dapper little creature imaginable. Each one brought a present for Thumbelina, but the best of them all was a pair of beautiful wings from a large white fly. These were fastened to her back, so that she too could flit from flower to flower. There was such rejoicing, and the swallow sat up above in its nest and sang for them as well as it could, but the poor bird was really too sad at heart, for it was very fond of Thumbelina and would have liked never to be parted from her.

"You shan't be called Thumbelina", said the guardian spirit of the flower to her. "It's an ugly name, and you are so pretty. We will call you Maia."

"Goodbye, goodbye," said the swallow and flew away again from the warm countries, far away back to Denmark. There it had a little nest above the window where the man lives who can tell fairy tales, and there it was that the swallow sang "tweet-tweet!" to him . . . And that's where the whole story comes from.

80

The Emperor's New Clothes

Many years ago there lived an Emperor who was so tremendously fond of fine new clothes that he spent all his money on being elegantly dressed. He took no interest in his army or the theatre or in driving through the country, unless it was to show off his new clothes. He had different clothes for every hour of the day and, just as you might say of a King that he was in the council-chamber, so it was always said of the Emperor: "He's in his wardrobe."

There was plenty of fun going on in the city where the Emperor lived. Strangers were continually arriving, and one day there came two swindlers. They made out they were weavers and could weave the very finest stuffs imaginable. Not only were colours and design unusually attractive, but the clothes made from their material had the peculiarity of being invisible to anyone who wasn't fit for his post or who was hopelessly stupid.

"I say! They must be wonderful clothes," thought the Emperor. "If I had some, I could find out which of my statesmen were unfit for their posts and also be able to tell the clever ones from the stupid. Yes, I must have some of that stuff woven for me at once." And he paid down a large sum of money to the swindlers straight away, so as to enable them to start work.

And they did; they put up a couple of looms and pretended to be

working, although there was absolutely nothing in the loom. They coolly demanded the most delicate silk and the finest gold thread, which they promptly stowed away in their own bags; and then they went on working far into the night at their empty looms.

"Well, now, I wonder how they are getting on with the work," said the Emperor to himself. But there was one point that really made him feel rather anxious, namely, that a man who was stupid or quite unfit for his post would never be able to see what was woven. Not that he need have any fears for himself—he was quite confident about that—but all the same it might be better to send someone else first, to find out how things were going. Everyone in the city had heard of the mysterious power possessed by the material, and they were all eager to discover how incapable or stupid his neighbour was.

"I'll send my honest old Prime Minister to the weavers," thought the Emperor. "He's the best one to see what the stuff looks like, for he has plenty of sense and nobody fills his post better than he does."

So off went the honest old Premier to the workshop where the two swindlers sat busy at their empty looms. "Lor' bless my soul!" thought the Minister with eyes starting out of his head. "Why, I can't se anything!" But he was careful not to say so.

The two swindlers begged him to take a closer look—didn't he find the colours and design most attractive? They then pointed to the empty loom but, although the poor old Minister opened his eyes wider and wider, he couldn't see a thing; for there wasn't a thing to see. "Good Lord!" he thought, "Is it possible that I'm stupid? I never suspected that, and not a soul must hear of it. Can it be that I'm unfit for my post? No, it will never do for me to say that I can't see the material."

"Well, what do you think of it?" asked the one who pretended to be weaving.

"Oh, it's charming! Quite exquisite!" said the old Minister, looking through his spectacles. "What a pattern and what colouring! I shall certainly tell the Emperor how pleased I am with it."

"Ah, we're glad to hear that," said the swindlers, and they then gave details of the colours and the peculiar design. The old Minister listened carefully, so as to be able to repeat all this when he came back to the Emperor—which he duly did.

The swindlers now demanded more money, more silk and more gold thread, for these would be required for weaving. They put it all into their own pockets—not a thread came into the loom—while they went on working the empty frames as before.

By and by, the Emperor sent another honest official to see how the weaving was getting on and whether the stuff wouldn't soon be ready. The same thing happened to him as to the Minister: he looked and looked but, as nothing was there but the empty looms, he couldn't see anything.

"There, isn't it a handsome piece!" said the swindlers, as they pointed out the beauty of the design which wasn't there at all.

"I know I'm not stupid," thought the man, "so it must be my fine position I'm not fit for. Some people might think that rather funny, but I must take good care they don't get to hear of it." And then he praised the material which he couldn't see and assured them of his delight in its charming shades and its beautiful design. "Yes, it's quite exquisite," he said to the Emperor, when he got back.

The splendid material became the talk of the Town. And now the Emperor himself said he must see it while it was still in the loom.

Quite a throng of select people, including the two honest old officials who had been there already, went with him to where both the crafty swindlers were now weaving for all they were worth without the vestige of a thread.

"Look, isn't it magnificent!" said the two honest officials. "If your Majesty will but glance—what a pattern, what colouring!" And they pointed to the empty loom, feeling certain that the others could see the material.

"What's this?" thought the Emperor. "I can't see anything—this is appalling! Am I stupid? Am I not fit to be Emperor? This is the most terrible thing that could happen to me . . . Oh, it's quite wonderful," he said to them; "it has our most gracious approval." And he gave a satisfied nod, as he looked at the empty loom; he wasn't going to say that he couldn't see anything. All the courtiers who had come with him looked and looked, but they made no more of it than the rest had done. Still, they all said just what the Emperor said—"Oh, it's quite wonderful!"—and they advised him to have some clothes made from this splendid new material and to wear them for the first time in the grand procession that was shortly taking place. "Magnificent!" "Delightful!" "Superb!" were the comments that ran from mouth to mouth; everyone was so intensely pleased with it. On each of the swindlers the Emperor bestowed a knighthood, with a badge to wear in his button-hole, and the title of Imperial Weaver.

On the eve of the procession the swindlers sat up all night with something like twenty lighted candles. People could see how busy they were finishing off the Emperor's new clothes. They pretended to take the stuff off the loom, they clipped away at the air with huge scissors, they worked at their needles without thread, and at last they announced:

"There! The Emperor's clothes are ready!"

Then the Emperor, with his most distinguished gentlemen-in-waiting, went in person to the weavers, who each put out his arm just as if he were holding something and said: "Here are the Breeches! Here is the Robe! Here is the Mantle!" And so on. "They are all as light as gossamer; you can hardly feel you have anything on—that's just the beauty of them."

"Yes, indeed," answered the gentlemen-in-waiting. But they couldn't see a thing, for there wasn't a thing to see.

"Now will your Imperial Majesty be graciously pleased to take off your clothes?" said the swindlers. "Then we can fit you with the new ones, there in front of the big glass."

So the Emperor took off the clothes he was wearing, and the swindlers pretended to hand him each of the new garments they were supposed to have made, and they took him at the waist as if they were fastening something on . . . it was the train, and the Emperor turned and twisted in front of the looking-glass.

"Goodness! How well they suit your Majesty! What a wonderful fit!" they all exclaimed. "What a cut! What colours! What sumptuous robes!"

The Master of Ceremonies came in with an announcement. "The canopy to be carried above Your Majesty in the procession is waiting outside."

"All right, I'm ready," said the Emperor. "Aren't they a nice fit!" And he turned round once more in front of the glass, for he really had to make them think he was gazing at his fine clothes.

The chamberlains who were to carry the train groped about on the

floor as if they were picking the train up; and, as they walked, they held out their hands, not daring to let it be thought that they couldn't see anything.

There marched the Emperor in the procession under the beautiful canopy, and everybody in the streets and at the windows said: "Goodness! The Emperor's new clothes are the finest he has ever had. What a wonderful train! What a perfect fit!" No one would let it be thought that he couldn't see anything, because that would have meant he wasn't fit for his job, or that he was very stupid. Never had the Emperor's clothes been such a success.

"But he hasn't got anything on!" sad a little child. "Goodness gracious, do you hear what the little innocent says?" cried the father; and the child's remark was whispered from one to the other.

"He hasn't got anything on! There's a little child saying he hasn't got anything on!"

"Well, but he hasn't got anything on!" the people all shouted at last. And the Emperor felt most uncomfortable, for it seemed to him that the people were right. But somehow he thought to himself: "I must go through with it now, procession and all". And he drew himself up still more proudly, while his chamberlains walked after him carrying the train that wasn't there.

Dad's always right

Now listen! I'm going to tell you a story I heard when I was a boy. Since then the story seems to have become nicer every time I've thought about it. You see, stories are like a good many people—they get nicer and nicer as they grow older, and that is so pleasant.

Of course you've been in the country, haven't you? You know what a real old farmhouse looks like, with a thatch roof all grown over with moss and weeds and a stork's nest perched on the ridge—we can't do without the stork—and crooked walls and low-browed windows, only one of which will open. The oven pokes out its fat little stomach; and the elder-bush leans over the fence, where there's a little pond with a duck or some ducklings, just under the wrinkled willow tree. Yes, and then there's a dog on a chain that keeps barking at all and sundry.

Well, that's just the sort of farmhouse there was out in the country, and two people lived in it, a farmer and his wife. They had little enough of their own, and yet there was one thing they could do without: that was a horse which used to graze along the roadside ditch. Father would ride it into town, the neighbours would borrow it, and of course one good turn deserved another; and yet they felt it would pay them better to sell the horse or to change it for something else that might be still more use to them. But whatever was it to be?

89

"You'll know best, Dad!" said his wife. "It's market-day today, so you just ride into town and get some money for the horse or else change it for something good. What you do is always right. Now ride along to market!"

And then she tied on his necktie—she knew how to do that better than he did—and she tied it in a double bow; it did look smart. And she brushed his hat with the flat of her hand and gave him a nice warm kiss, and then away he rode on the horse that he was either to sell or exchange. Yes, depend upon it, Dad knew.

There was a burning sun and not a cloud in the sky. The road was full of dust, there were such a lot of people driving and riding to market or going there on Shanks' pony. It was scorching hot, and there wasn't a scrap of shade on the road.

A man came along driving a cow—you couldn't imagine a finer cow. "I'll bet she gives lovely milk," said the farmer to himself, thinking what a good exchange it would make. "I say, you with the cow," he called out, "I'd like to have a word with you. Now look here, I suppose a horse is really worth more than a cow. But, never mind, I've more use for a cow. Will you change over?"

"You bet I will!" said the man with the cow. And so they changed over.

Well, now the deal was done, and the farmer might just as well have turned back. After all, he had done what he wanted; but then, you see, he had made up his mind to go to market, and so to market he would go, if only to have a look at it. So on he went with his cow. He quickened his pace, and so did the cow, and presently they found themselves walking alongside a man who was driving a sheep. It was a good sheep, in good condition and with a good fleece.

90

"I could do with that sheep, I could," thought the farmer. "It would find plenty of grazing at the side of our ditch, and in the winter we could bring in into the house. Really, when you come to think of it, we'd do better to keep a sheep than a cow. Shall we do a swop?" he asked.

Yes, the man who had the sheep was quite ready to do that; and so the bargain was struck, and the farmer went on with his sheep down the road. There, by a stile, he saw a man with a big goose under his arm.

"That's a plump'un you've got there!" said the farmer. "It's got both feathers and flesh; that'd look well if we kept it by our little pond. It'd be something Mother could save her scraps for. She's often said: 'If only we had a goose!' Well, now she can have one—and she *shall* have one! Will you do a swop? I'll give you the sheep for the goose— and a thankee as well." The other man said yes, he didn't mind if he did, and so they made the exchange; the farmer got the goose.

As he neared the town, the traffic on the road got bigger and bigger, there was a swarm of people and cattle, stretching over road and ditch right up to the toll-keeper's potatoes, where his hen was kept shut in so as not to take fright and go astray and get lost. It was a bob-tailed, good-looking hen, that winked with one eye. "Cluck, cluck!" she said. What her idea may have been, I can't say; but the farmer's idea, when he saw her, was: "She's the finest hen I've ever seen; she's finer than Parson's brood-hen. I could do with that hen, I could. A hen will always find a bit o' corn; she can almost take care of herself. I reckon it's a good exchange if I get her for the goose. "What do you say to a swop?" he asked. "Swop?" answered the other. "Why, yes, that's not at all a bad idea." And so they changed over; the toll-keeper got the goose, and the farmer got the hen.

He had done such a lot of things on his way to town, and it was a warm day and he was tired. He felt he could do with a drop to drink and a morsel to eat. He had now reached the inn and, just as he was about to enter, there was the ostler coming out, and he met him right in the doorway carrying a bag that was brimful of something.

"What's that you've got there?" asked the farmer.

"Rotten apples," answered the ostler. "A whole sackful for the pigs."

"Why, what a tremendous lot! I do wish Mother could see that. Last year we only had one solitary apple on the old tree by the coal-shed. That apple had to be kept, and it lay on the chest of drawers till it burst. 'That looks so prosperous', said Mother. Well, here's a prosperous sight for her—how I wish she could see it!"

"What'll you give me?" asked the ostler.

"Give? I'll give you my hen in exchange." And so he gave him the hen, got the apples in exchange and went into the taproom straight up to the bar. His sack with the apples he leaned against the stove, without noticing that the fire was alight. He found a number of strangers in the room—horse-dealers, cattle-dealers and two Englishmen; these two were so rich that their pockets were bursting with gold. And the way they bet—you just listen to this.

S-s-s! S-s-s! What was that they could hear beside the stove? "The apples were beginning to roast. "Whatever is it?" they asked. Well, they very soon heard. They were given the whole story of the horse which was changed for the cow, and so on right down to the rotten apples.

"Well, well! Your missus'll warm your ears for you, when you get home!" said the Englishmen; "there'll be a fine set-out."

"No, she won't, she'll give me a kiss," said the farmer. "She'll say: Dad's always right!"

"Shall we have a bet?" they asked. "Golden sovereigns by the barrel —a hundred pounds to the hundredweight!"

"Make it a bushel—that'll be enough," said the farmer, "I can only put up a bushel of apples, with myself and the missus thrown in. After all, that's more than full measure—that's heaped measure."

"Done!" they answered, and the bet was made.

The innkeeper brought out his cart; the Englishmen got in, the farmer

got in, the rotten apples got in, and soon they all came to the farmer's house.

"Good evening, Mother."

"Good evening, Dad'."

"Well, I've done the deal."

"Ay, you're the one for that," said the wife and, heeding neither bag nor strangers, she gave him a hug.

94

"I exchanged the horse for a cow."

"Thank goodness for some milk!" said the wife; "now we can have milk puddings and butter and cheese to eat. What a lovely exchange!"

"Well, but I swopped the cow again for a sheep."

"There, that's better still," she replied; "you think of everything. We've got plenty of grazing for a sheep. Now we can have ewe's milk and cheese and woollen stockings, yes, and woollen night-clothes—the cow couldn't give us that; it sheds its hair . . . You really are a considerate husband."

95

"But I swopped the sheep for a goose."

"My dear Dad, do you mean to say we shall have Michaelmas goose this year? You're always thinking how you can give me pleasure. What a lovely idea of yours! We can tether the goose and fatten it up for Michaelmas."

"But I swopped the goose for a hen," said the husband.

"A hen? That was a good exchange," said the wife. "The hen will lay eggs and hatch them out; we shall get chicks and a fowl-run. That's just what I've always wanted."

"Yes, but I swopped the hen for a bag of rotten apples."

"Why, now you must have a kiss," said the wife. "Thank you, dear husband o' mine. And now I've got something for you to hear. While you were away, I thought of a really nice meal to cook you when you got back: omelette flavoured with onion. I had the eggs, but no onions. So I went across to the schoolmaster's; they grow chives there, I know. But his wife's stingy, the mealymouthed vixen! I asked her to lend me —'Lend?' she repeated. 'Nothing grows in our garden, not so much as a rotten apple. I couldn't even lend you that.' Well, now I can lend her ten—in fact, a whole bagful! What a lark, Father!" And then she gave him a kiss right on the mouth.

"I do like that," cried the Englishmen together. "Always going downhill and never downhearted. It's worth the money." And with that they counted out a hundredweight of gold coins to the farmer who was not scolded but kissed.

Yes, it always pays for the wife to admit freely that 'Dad' knows best and that what he does is right.

Well, what do you think of that for a story? I heard it as a child and now you have heard it, too, and realize that Dad's always right.

96